Are You a Friend of Dorothy?

The **True Story** of an **Imaginary Woman** and the **Real People** She Helped

Are You a Friend of Dorothy?

The **True Story** of an **Imaginary Woman** and the **Real People** She Helped

Written by **Kyle Lukoff**

Illustrated by **Levi Hastings**

Simon & Schuster Books for Young Readers
New York London Toronto Sydney New Delhi

SIMON & SCHUSTER BOOKS FOR YOUNG READERS
An imprint of Simon & Schuster Children's Publishing Division
1230 Avenue of the Americas, New York, New York 10020
Text © 2025 by Kyle Lukoff
Illustration © 2025 by Levi Hastings
For information about special discounts for bulk purchases, please contact Simon & Schuster Special Sales
at 1-866-506-1949 or business@simonandschuster.com.
The Simon & Schuster Speakers Bureau can bring authors to your live event.
For more information or to book an event, contact the Simon & Schuster Speakers Bureau
at 1-866-248-3049 or visit our website at www.simonspeakers.com.
Book design by Laurent Linn
The text for this book was set in Filson Soft.
The illustrations for this book were rendered digitally with Clip Studio Paint on an iPad Pro,
using a combination of DAUB brushes and custom brushes.
Manufactured in China
1224 SCP
First Edition
2 4 6 8 10 9 7 5 3 1
CIP data for this book is available from the Library of Congress.
ISBN 9781665931663
ISBN 9781665931670 (ebook)

For Damon, Dave, and Jim, in the car to Ocean City
—K. L.

For Andrea, the Dorothy to my Rose—
thank you for being a friend, to the end of the rainbow
—L. H.

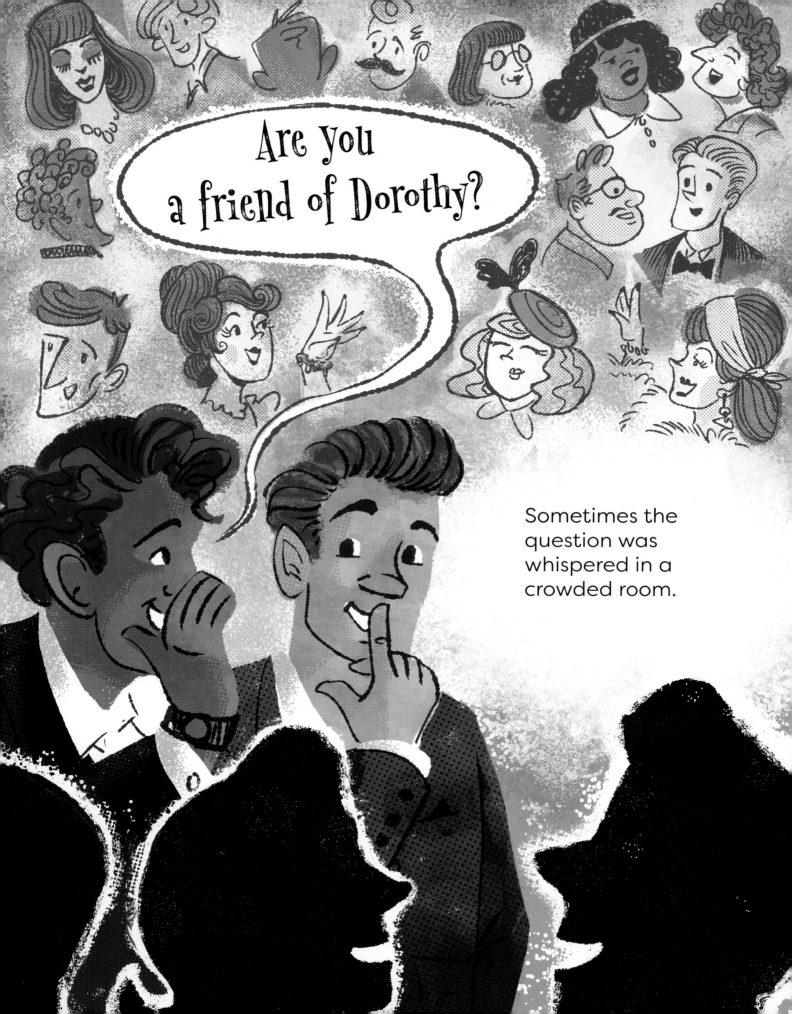

Sometimes the question was whispered in a crowded room.

Sometimes it was asked in private.

On a sidewalk or in a restaurant,

at a party or at work.

You see, people always know how to find each other.

And when it isn't safe to be out as yourself, you can always create ways to learn who your friends might be.

Not too long ago, in the United States of America, LGBTQ people—who were mostly called "gay" and "lesbian" back then—had to hide away that part of themselves.

There were laws that made it illegal to be gay. If a person's boss found out they were gay or lesbian, they could be fired.

If police decided that someone was wearing the wrong kind of clothes—men wearing dresses, or women wearing ties—they could be arrested.

If your family found out that you were gay, you might be sent to a hospital for a long time, and doctors would try to cure what they thought was a disease.

So LGBTQ people came up with ways to recognize one another that no one else would understand.

Special phrases and symbols, hints in handkerchiefs and in flowers. Like being in a secret club.

Outside you might be quiet and plain, but inside you could be bright and free. Surrounded by friends who saw who you really were.

But if the other man said,

Yes, darling, I am.

the two men would know that they were safe together.

Sometimes friends of Dorothy were allowed to keep their secrets. Other times, they were searched out.

Some people were especially unsafe. If you worked for the government or the military, you weren't even allowed to be secretly gay or lesbian. You could be spied on, hunted down, and fired, and might not be able to find a job again.

It was a hard and scary time for these communities, but there was still love and fun and friendship.

There were still parties and shows, dances and weddings. People still found who they belonged with.

But as whispers of Dorothy found their way around the country, they were overheard by ears that weren't in on the secret.

Undercover spies from the military were looking for gay service members, and some of them heard sailors call themselves "friends of Dorothy." And these spies started to whisper among themselves.

Who was this mystery person? How did she know all these gay men? Why did she know them? And how could they get her to reveal those secrets?

The officers went on a hunt for Dorothy. But they were searching for a woman who didn't exist.

No one knows for sure where the phrase came from, but it's probably related to Dorothy Gale, from Kansas. The girl in *The Wizard of Oz* has been important to generations of LGBTQ people for many reasons.

Dorothy dreamed of leaving her small town to find people who understood her, a story that many queer people can relate to.

Plenty of gay men were entranced by Judy Garland, the actress who played Dorothy in the popular film.

She was a talented, passionate performer who had a hard and sad life. And of course, the movie is awash in beautiful rainbow colors.

But Dorothy Gale wasn't a real person, so the officers weren't going to get her phone number anytime soon.

There was another Dorothy who might have inspired that phrase, but spies weren't going to find her, either. She was a famous writer named Dorothy Parker, known for being clever and grouchy.

She threw rollicking parties in the 1920s that many gay men and lesbians went to. There, you could talk to—or dance with—whomever you chose. And to get into one of her parties, you might say that you were one of her friends.

But Dorothy Parker died many years before the navy started looking for someone with her name. So of course they couldn't ask her anything.

OBITUARIES

DOROTHY PARKER

How did they look for Dorothy?

Did they call up every Dorothy in the phone book?

Did they knock on the doors of all the Dorothys they could find, demanding information?

Did they interrogate her "friends," trying to get one of them to crack and spill where Dorothy lived?

And what happened when someone, probably a very brave sailor, finally told them the truth?

We don't know a lot about this moment. But LGBTQ servicemembers probably laughed when they found out what had happened.

Their secret code had worked! Maybe a little too well. And the officers and spies who had made such a big mistake were probably pretty embarrassed.

A lot has changed in the United States of America since then.

It's not illegal to be gay or lesbian, in the military or outside it.

Millions of LGBTQ people have out and open lives.

There are movies and TV shows with happily queer characters. There are books and comics and musicals and art about queer people.

But sometimes it's still harder to be LGBTQ.

Some jobs might fire their queer employees for no good reason.

And some LGBTQ people have an extra-hard time finding jobs in the first place.

Some places have laws making it harder for transgender people to live openly as themselves.

And in many communities it's still not safe to come out.

LGBTQ people don't have to invent a secret language to talk about ourselves, but we still find ways of keeping each other safe.

We still know how to find our community. And learning about the ways we survived in the past could help people in the future.

There never was a Dorothy, but there will **always** be her friends.

"Gay and lesbian"?

You might have noticed that this book sometimes uses the words "gay and lesbian," and sometimes the acronym "LGBTQ." Sometimes it uses the word "queer." You might have wondered what these words mean, what the differences are between them, and why people might use one instead of the other.

The word "gay" often refers to a man who is attracted to other men. The word "lesbian" usually means a woman who is attracted to other women. When the events in this book took place, those words were commonly used to describe anyone who wasn't straight or cisgender. Another common word was "homosexual."

The acronym "LGBTQ" stands for lesbian, gay, bisexual (someone who is attracted to men and women, or people of many genders), transgender (which refers to diverse gender identities), and queer (which encompasses all the previous letters, and then some). We use this more often than "gay and lesbian" because it includes more people and more identities. Other versions of the acronym include other letters for other identities (intersex, asexual, pansexual), or the + symbol to indicate that there are even more. There's no *H*, though, because the word "homosexual" isn't used very often anymore.

There have always been people who have been attracted to, and fallen in love with, people who are the same gender as themselves. There have always been people who haven't followed their society's rules about gender. But the words used to describe these people are

"LGBTQ"? "Queer"?

as varied and diverse as the people themselves. Some words are old. Some words are new. Sometimes old words are rediscovered and used in a new way. And of course there are other words—and other identities!—in other languages and cultures.

If you know how someone describes themselves, you should use those words for them. If you're talking about groups of people who lived in a different time and might have a different understanding of themselves, it's okay to blend your knowledge of language today with how it was used back then. This book tries to honor both the reality of the past and the knowledge of the present, always with hope for the future.

Two history books for adults helped the author to write this book:

Coming Out Under Fire: The History of Gay Men and Women in World War II by Allan Bérubé

Conduct Unbecoming: Gays & Lesbians in the U.S. Military by Randy Shilts

Pictured on page 31, clockwise from the top center: RuPaul, Anderson Cooper, Shane Ortega, Bryn Kelly, Billy Porter, Megan Rapinoe, Danica Roem, John Waters, Kristen Kish, Mauree Turner, and Elton John.